There is no doubt that there are many Muslims on the crossroads or in a post Islam position, especially in Algeria. Social media is an incredible tool today, many are coming to faith via YouTube, Facebook and Christian TV Channels. I recommend this book for its insights and tools.

Rev Youssef Yacob (EPA Vice President Algeria)

Ben Adam has been and still is a rare combination of thinker, scholar, and compassionate friend-maker of Muslims, both during his years in Europe and the Muslim world. I'll never forget the gathering space he created where Muslims could ponder anything in a safe environment.

This small book *Encountering the World of Post-Islam* has riveted my thinking afresh as much as have any of the best thinkers who have given themselves to see Muslims love and follow Isa Al Masih. It says much more worth absorbing than so many longer but less applicable tomes.

Greg Livingstone, Doctor of Mission, Founder of Frontiers

This is a significant and helpful book and has been produced at just the right time. Many of us have recognised the increasing number of Muslims who are leaving Islam. Some are assuming they will be atheists, but many find that they can't abandon God and still have a spiritual hunger. This book makes many helpful observations, but is written in a spirit of humility, realising that there is not much firm data to go on, and that this is a reasonably new phenomenon influenced strongly by social media.

Bryan Knell, former director of Arab World Ministries UK, Founding Convenor of CRIB (Christian Responses to Islam in Britain) and author of The Heart of Church and Mission

I0895775

Ben Adam has given us an excellent resource in this book. His work on post-Muslims is well-researched and perceptive. If the insights of this work are put into practice widely and prayerfully, we can expect to see a fresh new influx into the church of those who have left Islam. May the Lord of the harvest use this for His glory.

Bernie Power, ThD, Lecturer in Islamic Studies,
Melbourne School of Theology, Australia

This is a creative and challenging approach to engaging with Muslims, which asks searching questions about how we share the Christian faith with Muslims. Ben Adam has for the last almost 20 years been pioneering this approach, with positive results. I recommend serious consideration of the approach outlined in this booklet.

Rev Canon Dr Phil Rawlings, Co-Director,
Manchester Centre for the Study of Christianity and Islam

REGNUM PRACTITIONER SERIES

ENCOUNTERING THE WORLD OF POST-ISLAM

Regnum Practitioner Series Preface

While we delight to serve the academic community, our mission is to enable the global church to engage more readily in God's mission in its very diverse contexts. To do this we seek to bring practitioners and academics together. Our desire is that this series will bridge the gap that sometimes exists between, on the one hand, Christian leaders and mission practitioners and, on the other, Christian researchers.

This book is published through a collaboration between MCSCI (Manchester Centre for the Study of Christianity and Islam), who prepared the manuscript, and Regnum Books.

mcsci

About the Author

Ben Adam has lived on different continents and had the opportunity to observe Islam in various forms and in a number of different countries. His life call has been to see churches planted among the unreached. This book comes from an observation of how Islam relates to the Great Commission to make disciples, and how it relates to the way we practice mission, particularly in fast-changing cultures.

In recent years, Ben Adam has been living in the UK, and has had the opportunity to observe how post-Muslims make a difference to the churches of Britain, as well as other countries in Europe and beyond. He has worked with others holding many different views of how churches should be planted in Muslim-majority areas. The inspiration for the book came from observing the gap between the ideal world of Islam and the Islam experienced by many who subsequently came to Christ.

ENCOUNTERING THE WORLD OF POST-ISLAM

Ben Adam

First published 2024 by Regnum Books International

Regnum is an imprint of the Oxford Centre for Mission Studies
St. Philip and St. James Church, Woodstock Road, Oxford, OX2 6HR, UK
www.regnumbooks.net

British Library Cataloguing in Publication Data
A catalogue record for this book is available from the British Library

ISBN: 979-8-8898-3889-0
eBook ISBN: 979-8-8898-3890-6

Typeset in Palatino by WORDS BY DESIGN

regnum mcsci

Distributed by Fortress Press in the US, Canada, India, and Brazil

Contents

Preface	1
Introduction	3
What is Post-Islam and Why Does it Matter?	5
The Rise of Post-Islam	7
The Biblical Idea of Ideological Struggle	13
Where and How Do We Find Post-Islam?	17
How does Post-Islam Help (or Hinder) the Message of the Gospel	21
Discipling the World of Post-Islam 1: Spreading the Message	27
Discipling the World of Post-Islam 2: Teaching them to Obey Everything	39
Conclusion	47
Bibliography	49

PREFACE

Several years ago, I first became aware of some of the debates about Islam among Christians in the UK. Some sympathised with the Muslim community and were quick to see the way that they had been misrepresented. Others were highly critical of Islam and regarded it as a threat to Western civilisation. Some held that interfaith dialogue would at least equip the church to reach out to Muslims with the Good News; others that a confrontational and critical approach was needed. Some emphasised friendship; others trained Christians to understand a Muslim world view. Some valued social programmes and support, such as help with language or homework classes. Others favoured literature production. For all the discussion and debate, none of these approaches seemed to lead to significant numbers of new believers in Christ. One leader involved in outreach to Muslims told me it was too early to say whether these approaches were fruitful. Yet they had been used for over 30 years by good, faithful, hardworking Christians.

All the while, people born into Islam were coming to Christ in increasing numbers. Yet what brought most of them to Christ seemed to have very little to do with any of our programmes to reach Muslims or train Christians. Most of the new Christians who came out of the baptism pools in the UK had not dialogued with Christians while they were Muslim. They had not had their Islamic ideas challenged face-to-face by Christians. The starting point of their journey was not usually a close friendship with a British Christian. What brought them to Christ was a spiritual hunger, and that spiritual hunger generally grew after they abandoned Islam. The journey out of Islam usually had nothing to do with Christians. What mattered was the next stage: what would happen when spiritually hungry and sometimes desperate people turned to the Christians nearby and asked for help. That is the topic of this book.

Introduction

There is a famous exchange in Conan Doyle's short story "Silver Blaze" between Sherlock Holmes and the Scotland Yard inspector Gregory Lestrade, who asks:

> *"Is there any point to which you would wish to draw my attention?"*
> *"To the curious incident of the dog in the night-time."*
> *"The dog did nothing in the night-time."*
> *"That was the curious incident," remarked Sherlock Holmes.*[1]

We think about what is, not what is not. Our eyes are trained to see features, our minds conditioned to remember events. Sometimes, the most important are not the things that happen, that jump out at us, but the things that do not exist. The gaps in the fence may be more important than the shape of the fence. So it is with Islam: there has been a great deal written about Islam from all kinds of points of view – political, social, religious, spiritual, and historical – and much less has been written about what happens when Islam withers.

Of course, military force or mob violence has been used to expel Muslims from Spain and India. Islam has been suppressed or co-opted by communists in countries such as Albania, Yemen, or China. But less has been written about what happens when those who have been raised in some kind of Islam simply leave it. We might notice them if they convert to another religion, but it suits very few people to watch over the no-man's land where no strong ideology reigns. It discomforts governments who wish to keep Muslims sympathetic.[2] It doesn't fit with great religious claims, which naturally focus on what people are, rather than what they are not. Post-Muslims rarely

---

[1] Arthur Conan-Doyle, *The Memoirs of Sherlock Holmes* (London: George Newnes, 1894): 22.

[2] Commonly through the government administration of the mosque foundations, or waqfs.

congregate, and only occasionally meet on small online forums dominated by sharp atheist rhetoric.

But it matters to Christians, not in and of itself, but because the large majority of those born into Islam who come to believe in Christ, do not come directly from conventional Islam. They pass through a period of doubt and questioning, and often totally reject Islam, before they come to understand or believe the gospel. Worldwide, the numbers of those who believe in Christ from a Muslim heritage is rising, often in step with a much wider group who reject Islam.

And yet Christians concentrate far more resources into speaking to those yet to question their Islam. In other words, we may be concentrating on the wrong part of the great mass of people who are born into Islam. Watching the religious rather than the irreligious may prevent us being effective in implementing Jesus' Great Commission to make disciples.

WHAT IS POST-ISLAM AND WHY DOES IT MATTER?

Post-Muslims are not 'bad' Muslims. For example, Muslims are over-represented in Europe's prisons. But just because the inmates have been convicted of a crime or two, does not make them post-Muslim. Indeed, Europe's prisons are breeding grounds for Islamic radicalism.[1] Muslims may drink, womanise, sell drugs, bet compulsively, never pray, never fast, and never go to the mosque. But this does not mean that they have ceased to be Muslims.

I will define a post-Muslim as one born or converted into Islam who no longer believes in its fundamental truth claims. There is obviously a vast range of opinions and attitudes within this slightly vague definition. It doesn't cover groups who call themselves Muslim, but who other Muslims do not recognise as Muslim.[2] Generally, these aren't post-Muslims. Even very liberal Muslims, who hold on to very little conventional Islam, still identify with the religion and people of Islam. There is an exception, however: the Quranis, or Quran-only Muslims. They believe that the hadith and other post-Quranic sources are unreliable,[3] and the text of the Quran is the only authoritative source. Even if they still call themselves

---

[1] Mubaraz Ahmed, "Prison Radicalisation in Europe", *Tony Blair Institute for Global Change* 17th August 2015, [Available at: https://www.institute.global/insights/geopolitics-and-security/prison-radicalisation-europe], [Last accessed: 6th February 2024].

[2] For the position on Quranists, see, for example: "Quranists, Islam's Outcasts", *Fanack*, 19th December 2019, [Available at: https://www.fanack.com/religions-in-the-middle-east-and-north-africa/islam/quranists-islams-outcasts/], [Last accessed: 6th February 2024]. Two thirds of Pakistanis do not recognise the Ahmedi sect as Muslim. Only 7% do: Neha Sahgal, "In Pakistan, most say Ahmadis are not Muslim", *Pew Research Center*, 10th September 2013, [Available at: https://www.pewresearch.org/short-reads/2013/09/10/in-pakistan-most-say-ahmadis-are-not-muslim/], [Last accessed: 6th February 2024].

[3] Daniel W. Brown, *Rethinking Tradition in Modern Islamic Thought*, (Cambridge: Cambridge University Press, 1999): 13, [Available at: https://ahadithstudies.files.wordpress.com/2010/12/brown-rethinking-tradition-islamic.pdf], [Last accessed: 6th February 2024].

Muslims, they are ready to think, to step away from traditional Islam, and to listen to the claims of Jesus in a way conventional Muslims are not. This is partly because the Quran itself encourages people to read and understand the Bible – the Torah, Psalms and Gospel,[4] and partly because no-one really knows what Islam would look like without either the traditions, which claim to record the words and actions of Islam's founder, or the schools of Islamic interpretation which bind every Muslim scholar.[5]

Our interest in the phenomenon of post-Islam is not neutral. It interests us because Islam is a factor in resistance to the gospel. Islam seems designed to block many of the key truth claims[6] of Christian faith: that God is One in the Father, Son and Holy Spirit, that Christ died for our sins, that he rose on the third day, that he sends his Holy Spirit so that we might be born again, that the word of God in the Bible is true. Incidentally, in some contexts, Islam does not seem to block such claims; for example, many say movements of Indonesia and Bangladesh meld Christian faith to Islamic forms and heritage.[7] In such a case, post-Islam becomes much less interesting to us. We are asking a question about making disciples. How can post-Muslims come to know and follow Christ?

---

[4] See, for example Surat Yunis, v94: So if you are in doubt, [O Muḥammad], about that which We have revealed to you, then ask those who have been reading the Scripture before you. The truth has certainly come to you from your Lord, so never be among the doubters (Saheeh international translation).

[5] Personal observation: in discussions with Qurani friends, patterns, including prayer patterns differ from conventional Muslims. Conventional Muslims, for example, assume five prayers a day are mandated by all Islamic texts. The Quran specifically mentions only three, as Quranis point out. See True Islam Website, "The Number of Salat authorised by God in the Quran", [Available at: www.quran-islam.org/main_topics/islam/pillars/number_of_salat_(P1200).html], [Last accessed: 6th February 2024].

[6] Muslims reject for example, God as Father, Jesus Christ as the Son of God, the death of Jesus and therefore the atonement on the basis of texts such as Surah Ikhlas 3, and Surah Nisa, 157. The validity of such interpretations is not as important as their widespread acceptance.

[7] See, for example Richard Croft, "Muslim Background Believers in Bangladesh: The Mainline Church Scene with these New 'Church' Members from Muslim Backgrounds", [No clear source], 2014), [Available at: www.academia.edu/16348999/Muslim_Background_Believers_in_Bangladesh_The_Mainline_Church_Scene_with_these_New_Church_Members_from_Muslim_Backgrounds], [Last accessed: 7th February 2024].

THE RISE OF POST-ISLAM

Obviously, post-Islam is nothing new. Throughout the centuries, Muslims like many others, have quietly doubted and abandoned their religion. Yet, there is something different about post-Islam in this generation. Post-Islam is usually not the movement from one religious community into another, as much as the movement away from any religious tribe. Newer, global and local factors contribute to its rise in this age.

One is the rise of information technology. Few governments can now effectively control information flow to their subjects. Levels of encryption in commercial software, easily available VPNs, the rise of satellite television and the change of information consumption to easily encrypted smartphones means that far more information is available, far more privately than ever before. People often learn ideas alone or in anonymous online communities. The space to develop ideas away from the surrounding culture has never been greater. Richard Dawkins' book *The God Delusion* was illegally downloaded 30 million times in Arabic, with three million downloads in Saudi Arabia.[1]

The skyrocketing levels of education across the world have only increased this information flow. Students across the world, including the Islamic world, are now routinely given access to learning tools that are easily turned against Islam. University education in Iran has expanded by over 1000% since the advent of the Islamic Revolution. Most university students are women. And those educational tools are liable to ask questions of Islam. In Germany, Sven Kalisch converted to Islam at the age of 15, and later became Professor of Islamic Studies in the University of Munster. Applying the sceptical theological tools he had learned from

[1] Florence Snead, "Richard Dawkins makes *God Delusion* free in Arabic to target Muslim countries", *i news*, 19th March 2018, [Available at: https://www.inews.co.uk/culture/books/richard-dawkins-to-make-god-delusion-free-to-download-in-arabic-136420], [Last accessed: 7th February 2024].

Christian theology, he concluded that Mohamed probably never existed, and shortly afterwards left Islam.[2]

Related to this, it is now far easier to view ideas in comparison with others. As a crude example, Islam has always made claims to provide an ideal society and political system.[3] Increased travel, globalisation and technology mean that few hermit kingdoms still exist. Islam's claims of greatness, and success, both now and in the past, are much easier to evaluate. Muslims have the ability to see, to imagine, and to understand the alternatives far more than ever before.

In addition, there is a growing movement in the West which not only emphasises political freedom,[4] but also the autonomy of the individual at a deeper level than any yet seen. Every individual can ask those around them to respect their self-definition of gender (and pronouns), sexuality, religion, or tribe. While obviously this thinking is contested even in the West, and translates poorly to the Muslim heartlands, it encourages the use of a space created by the individual without dominant narratives. It is a space where the individual stands outside a pre-determined identity, where they are not under the sway of a great religious power. A kind of watered-down postmodern existentialism challenges us to invent ourselves, and many Muslims take up the invitation, even if great numbers refuse it.

---

[2] Westfälische Wilhelms-Universität (WWU) Münster, "Neues Aufgabengebiet für Sven Kalisch", *Universität Münster*, 13th July 2010, [Available at: www.uni-muenster.de/news/view.php?&cmdid=5797], [Last accessed 7th February 2024].

[3] In Islamic history, the caliphs took over the political as well religious affairs of the Islamic state. See also, for example: Mabid Al-Jarhi, *The Islamic Political System: A Basic Value Approach* (Kuala Lumpur: INCEIF, 2016), [Available at: mpra.ub.uni-muenchen.de/72706/1/MPRA_paper_72702.pdf], [Last accessed: 7th February 2024].

[4] Ronald F. Inglehart, *Religion's Sudden Decline* (Oxford: OUP, 2021): 2. Inglehart's thesis is a dichotomy between pro-fertility religious norms, and choice-based secular norms. While elements of this thesis are unconvincing, the dichotomy between God-commanded behaviours and self-chosen behaviours is well documented.

There are no proper numbers for post-Islam, but David Garrison's book *A Wind in the House of Islam* gives some important clues.[5] In arguably the three biggest movements of Muslims to Christ in the last 100 years, there was a trigger which led people away from Islam.

In Indonesia, an uneasy relationship between communists, political Muslims, and the army fractured in 1965. The ensuing mass killing of communists left between 500,000 and a million dead.[6] The Indonesian government recognised only six religions, and many nominal Muslims, revolted by the massacres, registered as Christians. Muslim politicians had violated a principle of Indonesian life.

The same is true in Iran: the Islamic Revolution came to be seen, not as the legitimate expression of Persian identity in opposition to the West, but a violation of a Persian identity which was deeper, older, and more cultured than Shia Islam.[7]

In Algeria, the movement to Christ is helped on not only by the atrocities committed by the FIS but by an understanding of Amazigh identity that is not only not Arab, but also not Muslim.[8]

Recently, the rise of political Islam has scattered those questions from specific places and circumstances across the globe. Those questions appear in every news ticker, are pushed by adverts on social media and are forwarded in shared groups. The means of the rise of radical Islam are also the means of the rise in post-Islam.

Those media and information offer an Islam free of cultural baggage. They offer its application or enforcement, in purer forms, rejecting cultural traditions or political attempts to dilute the force

---

[5] David Garrison, *A Wind in the House of Islam: How God Is Drawing Muslims Around the World to Faith in Jesus Christ* (Monument, CO: Wigtake Resources, 2014).

[6] Mary S. Zurbuchen, "History, Memory, And The "1965 Incident" In Indonesia", *Asian Survey*, 42(4), 2002): 564–581.

[7] Shireen T. Hunter, *Iran, Islam, and the Struggle for Identity and Power in the Islamic Republic of Iran* ACMCU Occasional Papers Series (Georgetown, Washington DC: Alwaleed Bin Talal Centre for Muslim-Christian Understanding, 2014): 11.

[8] Carmen Garratón Mateu, "Religion et identité amazighe: réflexions sur le rôle de l'islam en Kabylie (Algérie)", in Mohand Tilmatine and Thierry Desrues (eds), *Les Revendications Amazighes Dans La Tourmente Des « Printemps Arabes »* (Rabat: Centre Jacques-Berque, 19th February 2018): Paragraph 45. The Amazigh are often called Berbers by outsiders.

of Islamic texts and authorities. Cultural Islam is quite capable of delivering general moralistic values that serve to keep society and families together.[9] However, when Islamic texts are read more literally, they produce a legal and social structure that many Muslims instinctively reject. For example, in Indonesia, a majority of Muslims would like to see sharia applied to the country. Of those in favour, however, most reject sharia punishments for crimes such as theft.[10]

Challenges to Islam are less likely to appear where it is diluted by political interference or a somewhat relaxed attitude to application. More radical Muslims, in these cases, can critique existing social forms as unislamic, and propose a more Islamic approach to rooting out social and political ills, just as Communists critiqued capitalism in the early part of the 20th Century. As long as it remains in opposition, those claims are unchallenged. But once in power, either in the family or in the society, Islam's claims are tested, and produce opposition. Many reject Islam. This was the case in Egypt, where the Muslim Brotherhood came to power after decades in opposition following the fall of Husni Mubarak. Massive opposition to the Muslim Brotherhood was followed by not only the fall of the Brotherhood from power, but a rise in non-religious attitudes in Egypt.[11] Equally, Saudi Arabia (ruled by an Islamic monarchy) has a high viewership of Christian satellite TV,[12] and a disproportionate

[9] General research on British Muslim families can be found here, for example: Kim Knott, "British Muslims: Families" *CREST*, 26th March 2018, [Available at: https://crestresearch.ac.uk/resources/british-muslims-families/], [Last accessed: 7th February 2024]. However, the way that liberal, as opposed to conservative, Islam binds families together is to some extent a personal observation.

[10] Pew Centre Report, "The World's Muslims: Religion, Politics and Society", *Pew Research*, 30th April 2013, [Available at: https://www.pewresearch.org/religion/2013/04/30/the-worlds-muslims-religion-politics-society-overview/], [Last accessed: 7th February 2024].

[11] Karin van Nieuwkerk, *Understanding Unbelief in Egypt*, Report on preliminary findings Radboud University, Nijmegen, The Netherlands, 2019, [Available at: https://research.kent.ac.uk/understandingunbelief/publications-2/understanding-unbelief-in-egypt/], [Last accessed: 7th February 2024].

[12] As per SAT7 Viewership survey December 2016: SAT-7, "New survey shows record number of SAT-7 viewers", December 2016, [Available at: www.sat7uk.org/press-new-survey-shows-record-number-sat-7-viewers/?cn-reloaded=1], [Last accessed: 7th February 2024].

number of Arab Muslims coming to Christ in the UK are Saudi.[13] Conservative Islam produces post Islam. Post Islam favours faith in Christ. Advocates of conservative Islamic reform and revolution are at the opposite end of the political spectrum from most Christians, and yet their actions favour an outright rejection of Islam and thus the spread of the gospel. When we pray for nations, we see the growth of conservative Islam in places like Afghanistan as a tragedy. Politically, this may be so. But it may be a crucial step in undermining the hold that Islam has on the people of Afghanistan.

[13] Personal observation.

The Biblical Idea of Ideological Struggle

The idea of powers that hold people in darkness is found throughout the Old Testament. These are spiritual powers, but they are not purely spiritual. Paul says:

> *[4]The weapons we fight with are not the weapons of the world. On the contrary, they have divine power to demolish strongholds. [5]We demolish arguments and every pretension that sets itself up against the knowledge of God, and we take captive every thought to make it obedient to Christ. [6]And we will be ready to punish every act of disobedience, once your obedience is complete. (2 Corinthians 10:3–6 NIV)*

Note that the strongholds are linked directly to arguments and pretensions – human thought forms that prevent obedience to Christ. As we will see, there is a direct link between prevailing forms of thought and the execution of the Great Commission.

The enemies of God in the Old Testament, equally, are not purely physical. We are often bewildered by the rhetoric of ancient Israel. The mocking, the scorn, the extended prophecies of the destruction of enemy nations,[1] or the violence of Israel's hatred of Babylon leave us cold. It seems unchristian and irrelevant. In order to understand it, we need to appreciate Israel's mindset and geography. Israel, and Judah to an even greater extent, were small states between the great powers of the day. The safety and prosperity of the state depended greatly on the weakness of the great powers around them. Judah would prosper when Babylon fell. God gives great promises to Israel in exile, that they would one day see the destruction of the city they called home.[2] Its power would be broken and they would leave. It was not Israel that would break the power of Babylon, just as it was not Israel that broke the power of Pharaoh, but God himself.

---

[1] See, for example Isaiah 13–23, Jeremiah 46–51, Amos 1–2.
[2] See, for example Zechariah 2:7.

The Messiah comes to overthrow all the powers that hold us. "For he has rescued us from the dominion of darkness and brought us into the kingdom of the Son he loves" (Colossians 1:13 NIV). This is the power of sin and death, and the power of the place where sin lives, the flesh. This power, the flesh, has a teaching department.

> *17 For the flesh desires what is contrary to the Spirit, and the Spirit what is contrary to the flesh. They are in conflict with each other, so that you are not to do whatever you want. 18 But if you are led by the Spirit, you are not under the law. (Galatians 5:17–18 NIV)*

When we read that the Messiah will rule the nations with an iron rod (Psalm 2), we understand not that he will kill the people of the nations; rather, that he will overthrow the gods of those nations, the teachings of those nations, and the worldviews that those nations represent.

Islam is well understood as one of those nations, and the increasing numbers of people rejecting Islam are well understood as those freed from the yoke of a powerful nation. But the overthrow of a hostile nation is no guarantee of freedom or prosperity for Israel. God overthrew Assyria, but the opportunity was wasted by Judah, as they failed to repent deeply, Assyria was replaced by Babylon, and Judah went into exile.[3] The same could be said of the overthrow of Egypt's power. Israel's release from external bondage never became real freedom for the generation who left Egypt. Internal bondage, a slave mentality, continued to hold them, so they died in the desert. In the same way, external forces, including false religious ideologies, can hold people in bondage away from the gospel. Encountering the world of post-Islam means taking the opportunities offered by the breaking up of a hostile power.

Equally, the breaking up of that hostile power might seem permanent when it was in fact only temporary. The Babylonians

---

[3] Thus Josiah is able to invite the Northern tribes to celebrate the Passover in the late 7th Century BC, and to destroy the altars at Bethel and other Northern shrines, in areas formerly under Assyrian control (2 Kings 23:15–23). Some 40 years later, Israel is in exile.

might leave, threatened by the Egyptians,[4] but they would be back. In many cases, it is the same with Islam. What appears to be a suspension of Islam, fades further when people begin to research other ideas. Marriage, children, life choices may harden hearts and fill the void left by Islam. The human heart abhors a vacuum. Just as Israel failed to take the opportunity of those gaps in their sieges, so the risk is that the church will miss the opportunity to speak into that vacuum before it is filled with non-Christian ideas.

---

[4] See Jeremiah 37:5.

WHERE AND HOW DO WE FIND POST-ISLAM?

Ceasing to believe in Islam is always an individual decision, but in common with other religious changes, it is strongly shaped by cultures and social movements. It is far more likely to happen in some environments than others. The collapse of Islam in Iran is more spectacular, in many ways, than the de-Christianising of Northern Europe. Every individual will come to their own conclusions, but the likely conclusions of an Iranian and, say, a Somali are different. In other words, we can think not only of post-Islamic individuals but also post-Islamic cultures.

The rejection of Islam is commonly linked not just to abstract questions of truth but to perceived or lived truth. That is, Iranians of all ethnicities are prone to reject Islam because they perceive it to have failed. Iran's Islamic rulers lack credibility and thus their message lacks credibility. Iranians are prone to make quite practical judgements about Islam, and the argument that a more radical form of Islam is needed seems impractical.[1] This is reflected too in Egyptian responses to the Muslim Brotherhood.[2]

Individuals are also prone to evaluate the truth claims of Islam through their own practical experience. If Islam delivers the goods of a happy, stable home life, a strong family structure and the opportunity to thrive, then people are much less likely to reject its truth claims. Conversely, if it produces an abusive and coercive environment, then individuals are more likely to reject it. I have known more than one post-Muslim who seemed to have forgotten the language of their home. Islam was bundled up with the language, memories and experiences of a dysfunctional household. Education and the information revolution make it easier for

---

[1] Ammar Maleki and Pooyan Tamimi Arab, "Iranians' Attitudes Toward Religion: A 2020 survey report", *Gamaan Website*, August 2020, [Available at: https://gamaan.org/wp-content/uploads/2020/09/GAMAAN-Iran-Religion-Survey-2020-English.pdf], [Last accessed: 14th February 2024].
[2] See van Nieuwkerk, *Understanding Unbelief in Egypt*.

individuals to evaluate their experiences and compare them with others, including non-Muslims.

Post-Islam can be silent in the sense that, while the person acknowledges to themselves or possibly to close friends, that they no longer believe Islamic teachings, they keep these opinions private. They are closet post-Muslims. Many suppress the tension between their religion and their lived experience. Their religion comes to have no practical bearing on their lives, and many simply avoid thinking about it. Often, they fear bringing the question to a crisis point of being forced to admit, even to themselves, that they do not believe. That acknowledgment carries with it threats to their family life, their marriage and friendship groups. In more Islamic countries, this admission carries with it the threat of violence or even death. For many, the cost of admitting that they do not believe is enough to push them into a passive acquiescence with Islamic forms without any genuine conviction.

We can state generalities of how people come to abandon Islam, but that does not mean that we will actually come into contact with them, let alone offer them the message of Christ. Post-Muslims tend to do the same things that Muslims do, except religious observance. They gather everywhere Muslims gather except religious spaces. I would speculate that they are more likely to live, work, or study at a distance from their families, as they forge a more independent path, but this is by no means always true.

The key to meeting post-Muslims and offering them the Good News is little different from the task of reaching out to others in our workplaces, markets, streets and shops. Francis Schaeffer was once asked how he would tell someone the gospel in an hour. He said that he would listen and ask questions for 55 minutes and then have something meaningful to say for the last five minutes.[3] People need prompting, encouragement, and a safe space to think out loud. In this specific case, they need a trigger to reflect on the gospel message. This doesn't mean that they need a long speech, but a short invitation, or a comment about God, church, or something spiritual.

---

[3] Francis A. Schaeffer, *He Is There and He Is Not Silent* (Carol Stream, IL: Tyndale, 2001): xxviii.

In other words, encountering post-Muslims is not a matter of specific techniques. It means going into spaces that might seem Muslim, or meeting people with Muslim names, and not assuming that the person is Muslim or is resistant to the gospel. It means not assuming we know what the other person thinks.

The main reason for this is that we might well miss an opportunity to reach out to someone with the gospel. But there is a second reason. Many post-Muslims are wary of religion and will tend to shrink from it. They often want a space where they won't be stereotyped and where they can speak freely. Therefore, when we treat people as Muslims, they may shrink from us, lose trust and see us as unsafe people, therefore would not share their deepest hopes, doubts, fears and questions. I remember one friend from the Middle East who had turned to me for relationship advice saying, "But Ben, I'm not a Muslim" when he thought my advice was too tinged with Islam!

The internet is one of the most obvious places to find post-Muslims, and it is a powerful one. One young woman renounced Islam so fervently that she turned to the internet for information about Christianity, on the grounds that anything which Muslims rejected so strongly probably had some good in it. She came to believe through watching Christian apologists. However, we will come back to the challenges and opportunities in the section below called "The teacher in the world of the internet".

How does Post-Islam Help (or Hinder) the Message of the Gospel

Opening the Way for the Gospel

Meeting post-Muslims doesn't mean that they will respond to the gospel, or that they will grow to maturity in Christ – the twin aims of disciple-making. In some ways, they are more open than most, and, in other ways, their journey out of Islam slows them down. We'll look first at why post-Muslims might be more open to the gospel than others.

Post-Muslims often have a well-developed moral sense. In fact, both Christians and post-Muslims seem to critique Islam on these grounds. Some of the most trenchant critics of Islam from Muslim heritage focus strongly on many issues well-known to secularists. They include women's rights, whether in property, marriage, or legal evidence. They might go deeper into the laws of war, plunder, concubinage, the laws of apostasy, or sharia punishments.[1] Unlike secularists, post-Muslims often understand that these moral objections need some proper grounding. Not only this, when they read the message of Jesus, they may be strongly attracted to his gentleness, his rejection of revenge, judgement, and condemnation, his way of addressing the heart, rather than teaching a controlling law. Mark Gabriel, for example, a former teacher of Islamic History at Al Azhar University, went through a period of depression after his studies stripped away his faith in Islam. He recounts his conversion thus: "My eyes fell on Matthew 5:38: 'You have heard that it was said, "Eye for eye, and tooth for tooth." But I tell you, do not resist an evil person. If someone strikes you on the right cheek, turn to him the other also.' My whole body began trembling. I had studied the Quran my whole life – not once did I find words as inspiring as this. I had come face to face with the Lord Jesus Christ. I lost all track of time. It felt as if I were sitting on a cloud above a

[1] See, for example, Ayaan Hirsi Ali, *The Caged Virgin* (London: Simon & Schuster, 2007).

hill, and in front of me was the greatest teacher in the universe telling me about the secrets of heaven and the heart of God. I could easily compare the Bible to what I had learned from my years of studying the Quran, and there was no doubt in my mind that I was finally encountering the true God."[2]

This links to a second feature of post-Muslims that differentiate them from many of their post-Christian peers. They are often theists.[3] Their rejection of Islam does not usually entail a rejection of God. They might be quite happy to accept that there is one good, creator God, who demands good from his creatures, but without imposing Islamic laws. This might make us think that the Old Testament had done its work, and that they were ready for the New. This may be true, but as we will see, it may not.

Post-Muslims are often searching. The loss of faith in Islam leaves a gap in meaning and purpose. The message of Jesus resonates strongly as a call home. It represents reconciliation to a God who they once feared. This may, possibly, be a factor in some of the intense spiritual experiences of post-Muslims. They are more likely to dream of Christ and react emotionally to the gospel than many ordinary secularists. Although God may give post-Muslims these dreams directly, it may also reflect a deep spiritual longing in their subconscious, welling up in the dream.

Post-Muslims are likely to be open to change. They have already undergone change, and taken a tough, uncomfortable choice. They are more likely to make the tough, uncomfortable choice to follow Jesus.

Post-Muslims commonly ask big questions about their own lives and the lives of their families. More traditional immigrants and their communities in the UK are shocked by the insolence of British children and their indifference to their parents or any moral boundaries. Muslims are aware of the dysfunction of much British

---

[2] Mark Gabriel, "Mark Gabriel's Testimony (Islam)", *Arabic Bible Outreach Ministry Website,* [Available at: https://www.arabicbible.com/testimonials/egypt/1624-mark-gabriel-testimony.html], [Last accessed: 12th February 2024].

[3] See Ammar Maleki and Pooyan Tamim above. 78% of Iranians believe in God. Approximately half report losing their religion, and 43% do not report any recognisable religious affiliation.

family life. Post-Muslims are equally aware of the social and family problems of the UK, including its inner cities and social housing estates, but they come to a different conclusion: Islam is not the answer, but Christianity may be. Often post-Muslims look for role models to navigate British society, enjoying its freedoms and opportunities while avoiding the pitfalls of social and moral anarchy in the UK. Those role models may be Christian.

Hindering the Gospel

On the other hand, post-Islam may come with features that slow or prevent the acceptance of the gospel. Some Christians may place too much emphasis on a post-Muslims' rejection of Islam, as though the next step, of commitment to Christ, almost follows logically. It doesn't.

Post-Muslims often hold to a moral plan based partially on Islam, and partially on human instincts. They tend to the conclusion that God loves good people and doesn't love bad people, even if they would no longer define good and bad people according to Islamic principles. This means that, not only that they are open to other religions which teach theistic moralism, such as the Jehovah's Witnesses, but they struggle to understand the gospel. Christian ideas, such as that humans are in slavery to sin, that they need salvation, that life is not a test, but that the Kingdom of God comes to those who believe is as counter-intuitive to post-Muslims as it is to Muslims.

To put this another way, a feature of Jesus' message is salvation. For post-Muslims, the search for an ordering of the world means a search for a right, human ordering. The gospel is not such an ordering. A brief look at the Sermon on the Mount would be enough to convince a post-Muslim that that such an ordering is not the primary goal of Jesus' teaching or actions.

Post-Muslims have a religious worldview that is widely shared with other theists – that God is teaching people wisdom for living. Religion will reveal a good, wise, productive, and fruitful life. Whether or not they believe in a day of judgement, a place of punishment or mercy, post-Muslims are likely to believe that the wise and productive religious life will be visible on earth.

This view, that the job of religion is to teach us wisdom for living, is related to another feature of post-Muslim religion. It is not only man-centred in the way that it conceives moral duty, it also tends to be self-centred. Religion answers the question "how should I live?" not just morally, but practically. What makes us happy is, therefore, likely to be the best religion. It's a feature shared with other therapeutic expressions of faith. In Christianity, these include lighter forms of prosperity teaching, and such gentler, man-centred teaching is gaining ground in Islam.[4] Again, although a form of Christianity works with this aspiration for happiness and a better life, it runs quite against the flow of the gospel. In some ways, the message of the gospel has more in common with radical Islam at this point than it does with much of the post-Islamic worldview. Osama bin Laden is supposed to have said after 9/11: "we love death as you love life"[5] – an idea which is much closer to Jesus' idea of taking up the cross, hating our own lives, or dying as a seed to receive life than it is to a softer, aspirational, comfortable religion which "works" for its practitioner.

Most post-Muslims may therefore hesitate to commit fully to Jesus. The percentage of post-Muslims in any given ethnic community varies hugely. In the UK, post-Muslims are more commonly found in refugee populations and younger people who are commonly the children or grandchildren of South Asian immigrants. But, while in popular imagination those who renounce Islam must already be highly committed and ready to run considerable personal risks, many post-Muslims are quite adept at taking the line of least resistance. And the gospel is not the line of least resistance. This can continue after conversion. While many

---

[4] For example, Mufti Menk, a leading Zimbabwean Islamic scholar, has backed up his twitter feed with a book called *Motivational Moments*. Mufti Menk, *Motivational Moments*, 1st edition (Singapore: ALQ Creative, 2020).

[5] There are a number of variants of this quotation, which would in any case have been delivered in Arabic. One version, along with other similar quotations can be found here: George W Bush White House Archives, "In Their Own Words: What the Terrorists Believe, What They Hope to Accomplish, and How They Intend to Accomplish It", 5th September 2006, [Available at: https://www.georgewbush-whitehouse.archives.gov/news/releases/2006/09/text/20060905-7.html], [Last accessed: 12th February 2024].

Iranians have been baptised, not many have left Western Europe or North America to work longer term in reaching Iranians in Central Asia or the Middle East. Syrian refugees who come to Christ in the Middle East are more likely to continue their journey to the US, Europe and Australia than to return as missionaries to the Arab world. Of course, we might also ask what proportion of Western Christians have undertaken risky and costly mission in such countries, but the point is that post-Muslims are not necessarily different from Westerners in also being averse to great commitments.

Christianity may appeal to post-Muslims as part of a conflict of worldviews. That is, if the Muslim world is seen as dysfunctional, corrupt and underpinned by a violent and backward religion, the ways of the West are to be preferred. The religion of the West allows a well-functioning state and society to operate with democratic ideals and a progressive, tolerant worldview. Christianity may be seen as that religion. Ayaan Hirsi Ali recently announced her conversion to Christianity, saying "Atheism cannot equip us for civilisational war."[6] There she says, "As Tom Holland has shown in his marvellous book Dominion,[7] all sorts of apparently secular freedoms — of the market, of conscience and of the press — find their roots in Christianity." This might be true, but Western evangelical Christians know that, while Christianity may have contributed to the creation of high-functioning democratic states, it now contests many of the claims of modern post-Christian society. We no longer see ourselves as the religious arm of a civilising project. Unique truth, sexuality, abortion, and other issues draw Christian faith into conflict with the political structure it helped to create. For some post-Muslims, the gospel then conflicts with a culture that they have chosen as a model of tolerance.

Post-Muslims are often quite sceptical of all religious claims. They may have abandoned Islam by soaking up information from

---

[6] Ayaan Hirsi Ali, "Why I am now a Christian", *Unherd Club*, 11th November 2023, [Available at: https://unherd.com/2023/11/why-i-am-now-a-christian/], [Last accessed: 12th February 2024].

[7] Tom Holland, *Dominion: How the Christian Revolution Remade the World* (London: Little Brown, 2019).

non-Muslim sources. That means that, when they research Christianity, they are unlikely to simply turn to Christian sources. They are quite likely to have come across Muslim and secular critiques of the Bible. One (very angry) young Kurdish man I spoke to in the UK had weak English, but he had heard of 1 Samuel 15, where Samuel orders the annihilation of the Amalekites. Post-Muslims are likely to have come across critiques of the Bible as self-contradictory, inaccurate or corrupt. We do not monopolise the flow of information to them.

DISCIPLING THE WORLD OF POST-ISLAM
1: SPREADING THE MESSAGE

The next question is the crucial one for the church. What matters to us is not what is but what could be. Under Jesus' call to execute the Great Commission, our question is: how can we lead post-Muslims to Christ? The "we" here is the whole church. The work of evangelism to post-Muslims will not, in the main, be done by highly skilled or aware professionals. It will be achieved by family members, work colleagues, teammates, and classmates. Reaching post-Muslims is, in the main, a similar task to reaching post-Christians, or agnostics, or post-Buddhists. Its fundamentals are the same, only details differ.

The most obvious way to reach post-Muslims is, quite simply, to tell them the gospel. In most ways, this is the truest and most useful answer. Every decision to follow Christ is a reaction to the gospel. If we want people to follow Christ, we must tell them the gospel, and expect an answer. Post-Islam does not interest us as a sociological phenomenon, it interests us only insofar as it affects the responses to the claims to Jesus. Therefore, the simplest way to test responses to the claims of Jesus is to communicate those claims. Post-Muslims are different from others largely because of our assumptions about them. We sometimes hesitate to tell the gospel to people we think might be Muslim. We fear the impact on our friendship or worry about seeming rude. We may even fear the impact that accepting the gospel will have on their family lives. Some years ago, I became intrigued by the idea of equipping young people to share the gospel with their Muslim peers. I shared this idea with a staff worker of a Christian organisation working on an interfaith project. He became angry, and shouted, "what about 'honour your father and mother?'" We may count the cost of following Christ for people, and hesitate to share the good news, rather than allowing them to count the cost and choose for themselves. We might believe that they will not be interested in our church's carol service, or wouldn't come to an

Alpha course, so we don't invite them. We end up discriminating against people with Muslim names because of the assumptions we make.

Although we often fail to speak, we can also miss opportunities with post-Muslims because we don't listen to them, or give them the chance to tell us what they really think. It's important to keep listening; people change, as the Holy Spirit works. One of them put it to me this way: "when you first spoke to me, I wasn't ready. I couldn't hear it. Now I'm ready." Another post-Muslim who came to Christ stopped me on the street to apologise for haranguing me when I'd spoken to her about a year before. She described her heart as being like the soil of the parable of the sower. It had changed. Post-Muslims, by definition, have changed their minds. They're also much more likely to say different things in front of different people.

Both speaking and listening come out of love. Of course, this is a basic principle of telling people the gospel but, here, there is a twist. Post-Muslims often feel that they don't have a safe space to tell people what they're thinking. In fact, most human beings feel like this a lot of the time. And leaving Islam carries with it conflicting emotions, including anger and even guilt. They might have rejected Islam, but that doesn't mean that they trust someone to draw them into a new religion, where they might be burnt again. Post-Muslims, more perhaps than others, need to know that we genuinely care about them before they will trust us. We can communicate that in many subtle ways, and some not so subtle, such as hospitality and generosity.

In Manchester and London, there are a number of retail platforms set up to reach out to all kinds of people. These include bookshops and market stalls. One of the great virtues of retail is that it puts the customer first. The shop's decor might speak of beauty, peace, and order, but the customer is in charge of every conversation. The very shape of the encounter gives every visitor the chance to express themselves, and it gives the opportunity for everyone to tell us something of their story. It fits the pattern that we should be quick to listen and slow to speak because most post-Muslims need time, space and confidence to talk about their journey, and to begin to consider the gospel. From that space, we are able to speak to people, to encourage them and to invite them to activities, meetings and events. The pace might sometimes seem slow, but over the years, it produces a steady impact which seems to exceed that of more spectacular street evangelism.

THE MESSENGER

This next part is about where we choose to work, and how we hold ourselves out to the world. For most people, work, study or marriage are the things that hold us to our place and society. Those things feed us, our friends, and shape our ministry. Some people choose to live and offer Christ in places that are largely Muslim or post-Muslim, whether that is in the UK or elsewhere. The next section is mostly about how we make those choices – how we position ourselves to be effective as servants of the gospel.

A lot of writing about reaching Muslims has been based on the idea of friendship as a bridge. Given that Muslims do not understand Christianity or trust Christians, the argument runs, we must build trust in order to communicate the gospel. That trust is based on friendship, and so that is our starting point. Roland Muller in his excellent book, *The Message, the Messenger, and the Community*[1] argues that this is bad friendship and bad evangelism. The friendship is tinged with an agenda, and yet the evangelism is limited by the need to maintain the relationship. He argues that evangelists should take the position of the "teacher", one whose identity is bound up with that of the message. This does not preclude friendship, but it frees the evangelist to do their work. Muller writes primarily to those working among Muslims, but his ideas are, if anything, more applicable to post-Muslims.

Most of those born into Islam are still Muslim. Most of those who have left Islam are not particularly interested in following Christ. But some are. Evangelism among post-Muslims means being "findable". If someone wanted to come to Christ, would they have an avenue to do that? This is where the "teacher" becomes important. As a semi-public figure who speaks the words of Christ, he needs to be accessible to the spiritually hungry. One family I

[1] Roland Muller, *The Messenger, the Message, the Community: Three Critical Issues for the Cross-Cultural Church-Planter* (Vancouver: CanBooks, 2006).

know had a huge influence on their church. They came into the church through a long web of relationships. The mother of the family had experienced a miraculous encounter with Jesus. The family's neighbours were a young couple in an Islamic marriage. The wife in this Islamic marriage was a nominal Muslim, and her husband not a Muslim at all. Her "husband" had been introduced to someone from the church through a local African Christian who had come to a stall selling Bibles. Thus, a young woman in an Islamic marriage put the church in touch with the family, because she wanted to help the family convert to Christianity! Our goal is not so much to be change agents at the beginning of the process where people are still gripped by Islam – good and useful although that is – as much as delivering the message of Christ at a later stage in the process. The earlier part of the process, rejecting Islam and looking for other answers, is something that happens in the background, before we even meet the person.

If this is true, why is it that it seems to be counter-intuitive? In the UK, we have become used to multiple resistant cultures. We might believe that pre-evangelism is our primary task. Or it might be, for some, that we fear the shame of being the teacher, outside the approving confines of the church. The position of the teacher is something that goes with our identity. Paul says:

> *For when I preach the gospel, I cannot boast, since I am compelled to preach. Woe to me if I do not preach the gospel! If I preach voluntarily, I have a reward; if not voluntarily, I am simply discharging the trust committed to me." (1 Corinthians 9:16–17 NIV)*

Of course, it might be that we are simply friends with Muslims. We have not befriended them to preach the gospel. It is the genuine give and take of normal human companionship. This is, of course, a good thing. But the teacher of the word presents himself as a servant of the word in all circumstances. The shame which may follow is a natural consequence of following Christ: the cross is a place of shame, as much as physical and spiritual pain. This is why Jesus immediately draws the link between shame and following him.

What good is it for someone to gain the whole world, yet forfeit their soul? Or what can anyone give in exchange for their soul? If anyone is ashamed of me and my words in this adulterous and sinful generation, the Son of Man will be ashamed of them when he comes in his Father's glory with the holy angels. (Mark 8:36–38 NIV)

The Teacher in the World of Dislocation

Post-Muslims have left a spiritual home, and have not yet arrived at another. Some, of course, might end up as communists or nominal Zoroastrians, but many have no "thought community", and often limited community of any kind. They cannot identify with their heritage of upbringing, but they may not identify with other markers of community and shared codes that most people build up in their childhood and adolescence. There is a search, then, for "home". We can think of post-Muslims as belonging to a third culture – not their culture of origin, not the majority culture of the country they live in, but one marked by exile. That has significant consequences for how we make disciples of post-Muslims.

It might be that post-Muslims appear in churches with fairly homogenous cultures. They become cultural outsiders in the church, and they will then need insiders to help them join fully. You could use some resources on this, such as "Joining the Family",[2] which gives an excellent analysis of the kinds of churches which work for those of Muslim heritage. There is a subtle but important difference in understanding a church for post-Muslims and those for "believers of a Muslim background." Although similar, an understanding of post-Islam focuses not so much on the Islamic background, but on the nearer background, which is uncertainty, a lack of community, an identity in flux, rather than the Islamic heritage itself. Those features of identity change and displacement also hold true for people of other cultures – say post-Buddhist, or post-Sikh. The churches that work best for post-Muslims also work best for any diverse church where people come to Christ through flux, change and challenges to identity. The same factors which produce post-Islam are driving all kinds of identity change all over the world, but particularly in multi-cultural cities. Those cities have their parallels

---

[2] Tim Green, *Joining the Family* (Birmingham, UK: Kitab / Interserve, 2016).

in the cities of the old multi-ethnic empires of the Bible: Babylon, Rome, Antioch.

Most Muslims, and post-Muslims, do not live in the suburban strongholds of the British evangelical church. They are more likely to live in the cities where the white majority churches are weakest.[3] This is not to say that there are not strong churches in the inner city, but they are often African or Asian, rather than majority white British.

The likely spiritual home of many post-Muslims will not be a house built by one culture. It may well be a house built by many exiles, where the church lacks a single, central culture. However, this is still somewhat speculative. Currently in the UK, there are some signs of this, but the data is both sparse, and to some extent biased by the large number of post-Muslim Iranians coming to Christ. In any case, we will return to the gathering patterns of post-Muslims later, and what the church can learn from them.

Reaching post-Muslims is a task taken on by both insiders and outsiders. The outsider is one from a non-Muslim heritage who reaches out to his neighbours. The insider is the post-Muslim evangelist. Post-Muslim evangelists are often not the paragons of piety that we imagine. Evangelism among post-Muslims might seem like a high-risk, bold endeavour, only for the most committed. In fact, post-Muslim evangelists are often marked by other traits. They are often social, so they know a lot of people. They are often unmarried or without children. They can be reckless and have little regard for their reputation. Their message is often one that most mature Christians would avoid: Islam is evil, nonsense, destructive. Christianity is a better religion. One of the most active evangelists to post-Muslims I know was not even Christian: he knew a lot of Iranians and nagged them relentlessly to go to church. He did this, not out of obedience to Christ, but because he loathed Islam and was happy to see people leave it. The issue is how those evangelists or

---

[3] This view should be nuanced. Iranians, for example, are often housed in poorer areas as asylum seekers, but move towards suburban areas over time. Equally, highly educated middle-class Muslims might well rethink simpler religious ideas. Data on education, residence and language for the 2011 census can be found at datashine.org.uk. 2021 data are not available yet at this level of detail.

message-spreaders can be integrated into a church, a place of love, peace, and faith in Christ. The disordered world of the post-Islam message-spreader must somehow meet the temple of the Holy Spirit. We will come back to some of these challenges in the section "The church for post-Muslims."

The Teacher in the World of the Internet

One friend who works in an almost entirely Muslim country once told me, "We don't do much evangelism. The TV does that." This surprised me, as he was a cultural insider, far better able to reach non-Christians than others who did see their job as evangelism. What he meant was that their time was taken up by referrals from those who were watching Christian TV channels. In other words, the early stages of the search for Christ happened without him. In the privacy of people's own homes, they could try Christian satellite channels and react to them. The seekers would then contact the TV channel, who would then put my friend in touch with them. He would then contact them, or drive around his city, visiting people or bringing them to church.

Increasingly, people are not confronted with information as reality, as much as fed information for their consumption. The websites and platforms we use know us, our tastes and desires, and offer us the information that we might want. If you want to believe that Islam promotes equal and monogamous marriage, then look no further than your own Instagram feed. Knowing your deepest desires, it will help you to live in that world. That applies equally to post-Muslims. There are strident, angry post-Muslim forums, of course. But if someone loses interest in Islam and begins to seek out alternatives, Google, Meta and TikTok will know before anyone else. It will help you "get into what you're into."

The question is how the teacher should position themselves in such a situation. One answer is offline. Most post-Muslims in the West, at least, are perfectly at home on the internet, but at the same time are wary of its claims. They are sceptical of the abstract truth claims made online. This is accentuated by the yawning gap between Islam's theoretical claims made to educated non-Muslims and the reality of its practice and traditions. Young people were the least likely to engage with online churches in the pandemic. What they want is something genuine, human and not found on the internet, and this is, if anything, more true for post-Muslims, who tend to be socially dislocated, than it is for those still embedded in their community.

That said, there are ways of engaging online with post-Muslims. The first is to engage at the point of doubt. That is, those exploring the truth of Islam from within will ask a series of questions about the factual truth claims of Islam and its moral claims. Engaging with post-Muslims would do two things: it would engage those questions at the point where they are asked, and it would show the Christian alternative. These doubt questions could cover the nature of sharia law, the moral character of Islam's founder, the inconsistencies of the Quran and the hadith, the nature of paradise, and the path to it. Or it could involve suggesting content to someone looking at a book by a post-Muslim sceptic like Hirsi Ali, or even unorthodox Muslims such as Jalal ad-Din ar-Rumi.

I once read a woman's question to an imam on a comment thread. She said that she was looking forward to being in paradise with her husband and family. She asked how paradise could be paradise for her if her husband had two wives and the houris to distract him. The imam replied that she would be more beautiful than the houris and would have all the fine clothes and jewels she wanted, asking her if this answer satisfied her. "I'll think about it," she said. Christians can be present sometimes at this point in people's lives, where the problems of paradise, or sharia begin to weigh in on Muslims.

The gap between existing polemic content critiquing Islam and web content promoting Christianity is something that deserves a second look. That gap is content addressing those who have not yet begun to think seriously about Christianity, but no longer identify as Muslims. On the one hand, many post-Muslims are intelligent, rational people who know how to look for content on the internet and may not need specially targeted material. On the other hand, while sites like "Answering Islam" have excellent content, it isn't especially intuitive or visually attractive.

Cultural tags are often at least as useful. For example, because a majority of Iranians no longer identify with Islam, any content in Farsi is likely to find a strong response. The same could be said of the 47% of Tunisian youth who describe themselves as "non-religious" or the 19% of Saudis (of all ages) in the same position.[4] In an increasingly global world where artificial intelligence is making huge strides in machine translation, it is here perhaps that we might find the greatest return on internet content for post-Muslims.

In the UK, it is likely that the space for offering this content is smaller. We might look for a mismatch between heritage, expressed in a Muslim name, and social causes not commonly associated with Islam, such as socialism, vegetarianism, or environmental activism, but that kind of profile is more difficult to construct, and the impact of such targeted content is unproven.

A more proven track is a typical "unspammed channel" – building our social media profiles as followers of the Word should not be underestimated. The profiles of churches, ministries and individuals can be modified to reach seekers from a Muslim heritage.

Choosing Where Value is Found – Global Change

There is yet another dimension to choosing where we work. We might choose a city or a job, or we might even choose a country or a space. The next section points to ways that we can find the most open parts of the world – where post-Islam is spreading most quickly.

Post-Islam is not evenly distributed across the world – the winds of change blow where they will and throw up places and periods where Islam weakens and fades. Arabs and Arabic generate a lot of post-Islam. Muslims believe that God's language is Arabic. Some believe that the Arabic Quran is uncreated. When they say God said, "Be" to create the world, most believe he literally said, "Kun," the Arabic for "be". Islam is always an Arabising project. It teaches people that their prayers are only accepted in Arabic, that key religious ideas can only be communicated in Arabic, and the purest truth of the Quran can only be understood in Arabic. You could think of this as a form of religious and cultural imperialism.

---

[4] Zwemer Center, *Secularism is Drawing Muslims Away From Islam*, Zwemer Center Website, (undated) [Available at: www.zwemercenter.com/secularism-muslims-leaving-islam/], [Last accessed: 12th February 2024].

Under some conditions, the idea of Arabic as God's language becomes difficult to swallow. One day in the mountains of West Sudan, a young boy saw a European and took off running up the hill, as fast as he could. The European worker asked why. The Sudanese told him that he looked like an Arab to the boy, and that Arabs had burnt his village. In other words, at some points in the world, the Arabic religious project becomes associated with attempts to destroy other cultures, to invade or even enslave.

At this point, a gap emerges between someone's identification with their culture, and Islam. Islam is perceived as a hostile force, directed against a deeply held cultural identity. This can also be delivered by non-Arab Muslims, but when Arabs do so, it carries a particular force. This reaction against Arab-Islam opens the way for the gospel. It might be among the Fur people of Darfur, the Kabyle Berber of Algeria, or other ethnic groups of the Sahel.

How can Christians take advantage of this opportunity? The answer is not to complain about Islam. The reaction is already underway. It is to do what Christians have always done well: offering the gospel, the scriptures and literacy in local languages. These simple, necessary biblical things open heaven, where every language is represented, not just one. They allow people to find themselves again, and to meet God in the same way that He came to meet them: where they are. This might seem remote from the concerns of the UK. Even here, Christians are at work subtly undermining the pre-eminence of Urdu over Punjabi, Arabic over Kurdish, and Bangla over Sylheti. It's an example of knowing where to find "value" through the gospel in the culture of the heart, not ritual in the language of the oppressor.

Faith in Christ happens when the word of God is reinforced by the witness of the Holy Spirit. However, as we've noticed above, Muslims are held in a thought stronghold, called Islam. We've been looking not only at how that stronghold breaks down, but how we can be there when it does, and how we can support the work of the Spirit. One of the clearest indicators of a crumbling Islamic worldview is, as we've seen, Islamic fundamentalism. The more that Muslims deny political freedom, gender equality, and personal choice to citizens of Islamic states, the more Muslims will reject

Islam. That means that Islamic states deserve particular attention when looking for where Islam might be crumbling. For our purposes, genuine Islamic states will serve the purpose better than cultural Islamic states. Iran, Afghanistan and Saudi Arabia, are some of the most fundamentalist regimes in the world, and they are also some of the most open cultures to the gospel. Syrian refugees in Lebanon show a response to the gospel far in advance of anything known before the civil war.[5] If you look for a place to invest, then the most fundamentalist regimes of the world give us a clue. However, they are also the most repressive and hostile to the gospel. It can be easier to work with Afghans, Iranians and Saudis in the diaspora than it is in their homelands. Even here, however, there is a subtlety. The closer the work is to the point of alienation and disappointment with Islam, the more likely post-Muslims are to respond to the gospel. Syrians are more likely to accept Christ in Lebanon than they are in Germany, and more likely to respond to the gospel in Germany than they are in the UK.[6]

---

[5] Hikmat Kashouh, *Following Jesus in Turbulent Times* (Carlisle: Langham, 2018). Kashouh describes the rapid growth in Church of the Resurrection In Beirut on the influx of refugees from Syria.
[6] Kashouh, *Following Jesus in Turbulent Times.*

Discipling the World of Post-Islam 2: Teaching them to Obey Everything

The Church of Post-Muslims

If obedience to Christ can be thought of as following the greatest commands, to love God, other believers and our neighbours, all in slightly different ways, then it follows that the church is the testing ground for obedience. What kind of church works for post-Muslims? There is something of a riddle here, and one that applies more broadly to questions of church and culture. Those of a non-Christian religious heritage who come to Christ seem to choose, in multiple different contexts, to largely reject influences from their religions of heritage. Evangelical congregations in Catholic environments seem to have little Catholic influence, in Hindu environments, little Hindu influence, in Buddhist environments, little Buddhist influence. They seem to defy predictions that faith based on the Bible will adapt itself to contextual forms to produce something quite different from evangelical churches in other contexts.

This is also true of post-Muslim congregations. There is, as yet, little evidence that post-Muslims form churches in ways that are markedly different from other cultures. Visible, sustained growth in the church among post-Muslims suggests that churches bear a strong resemblance to those in other cultures. Where would we find this information? We would find it in the churches of Indonesia, Iran, Kabylia, Afghanistan, and others. As yet, just as we have little evidence that post-Hindu or post-Buddhist churches are forming a distinct church culture, we also have little evidence that visible post-Muslim churches are producing a distinct culture.[1]

---

[1] A text drawing on contextual theory might include Paul-Gordon Chandler, *Pilgrims of Christ on the Muslim Road* (Lanham, MD: Rowman and Littlefield, 2008). However, the structure and worship of Kabyle churches in Algeria or France, or Iranian churches in the diaspora are familiar to those of non-Muslim heritage. See Kathryn Spellman, *Religion and Nation: Iranian Local and Transnational Networks in Britain* (Oxford: Berghahn, 2005).

The contrary evidence at the moment, comes largely from highly contextual insider movements in places like Bangladesh or perhaps East Africa.[2] At the moment, it's hard to gather reliable data from such movements, because they're new, underground, or camouflaged against the underlying Islamic culture. In any case, they don't fit well into the category of post-Muslim, as there is little or no space between leaving Islam (if this has happened at all) and trusting in Christ as Lord. It's somewhat easier to observe the development of Trinitarian churches in post-Muslim spaces both in the countries of origin and the diaspora.

Of course, we could raise the objection that the evidence is gathered by conventional churches, and mirrors the prejudices of conventional churches. There are limits to this objection, however. Take the case of Iranian churches. They arise out of a Muslim Shia cultural background. They occur in multiple forms across many different cultures, and in different strands of Christianity, including Catholic and Evangelical. There is, in other words, plenty of space to create an indigenous church form. Yet, none of these forms, to my knowledge, bears much resemblance to Shia Islam.

That has implications for how churches for post-Muslims work. As so often, the clue is just doing the basics right. In Islam, the key community is not the mosque. The mosque, in Arabic, is a noun of place. It means where people bow down to pray. Blessing comes from praying in the mosque, but no interaction is required. The points of connection for Muslims are the family and the whole ummah of Muslims. One is much tighter than the church and the second much looser. So post-Muslims, in forming or joining churches, are often embarking on a new enterprise. It is not a family in that it is less hierarchical, and less intense. It is not a mosque in that there is a community with quite high expectations of one another.

The goal for the church among post-Muslims is to create a new identity. Obviously, this is a key goal of the whole church over

---

[2] See, for example, Rebecca Lewis, "Insider Movements: Honoring God-Given Community and Identity" in *International Journal of Frontier Missiology*, 26(1), (Spring 2009): 16–19.

history – to break down dividing walls, and to create a new humanity (Ephesians 2:11–22). There are, however, specific challenges and opportunities. Everything about growing Christians who have emerged from an Islamic heritage has to speak of grace – the wonderful reordering of the world around the mercy and goodness of Christ. The invitation to contribute gifts and service is not just the mark of a healthy organisation, it is the Holy Spirit shaping something entirely new. Muslim education is based, largely on a hierarchical transfer of information. The more knowledgeable educate the less knowledgeable. The church's development of gifts in love must speak of something quite different.

It is said that people with Muslim heritage have faced rejection and humiliation as they leave Islam to follow Christ. This is often, but not always, true of post-Muslims. It is also frequently, but not always, true that churches who offer a stronger community allow people who have been rejected by family and friends to find a new sense of belonging. However, we need to offer a word of caution here. Much of what we know of post-Islam in the UK is from those who arrived relatively recently as refugees. More than half of all post-Muslim Christians in Britain are Iranians, who routinely abandon Islam, with minimal social penalties in the UK, at least. Much of the sense of loss and alienation is caused by moving to the UK, seeking asylum, and trying to adapt to a new culture and language.

There is another wave of post-Islam growing across the world, as well as in the UK. These post-Muslims speak English as their mother tongue, and are quite at home in the UK, and often nowhere else. They are almost always employed or studying, and have good access to housing. This may well change the way that we lead churches which welcome post-Muslims, who have more money, better connections and less time than the first wave of post-Muslims who have moved into British churches.

Having said that, some of the old generalisations still hold true. Post-Muslims who come to Christ tend to be younger adults, and they, like many young adults, are looking for community. The most plausible church for post-Muslims will likely offer a different view of community, a different economic and social order, and offer a different vision of truth.

Many human structures tend towards hierarchy and the exercise of power – and this will easily translate into the church. The power of organising and teaching can easily become the dominant feature of churches, and the fear of chaos at the edge of society where change takes place can even accentuate this. In order to watch over the rapid spread of false teaching, immorality, drug use or mental illness, we might want a core of stable, well-organised people to lead the church. There is nothing wrong with this. The problem occurs where leadership becomes ministry. Service in the body of Christ is partly found in the judging and teaching roles of eldership. But it is also found in the unpredictable, fast-changing realm of the Holy Spirit, who gives gifts according to his will, not according to the recipient's worth or intelligence. Gifts of evangelism, prophecy, faith, healing or words of knowledge are breathed into the church as "manifestations of the Spirit"'. This Spirit-given order is quite different from human ordering, and quite different from the power structures of the mosque. This includes, as we have seen before, the gift of evangelism, where evangelists are often not leaders in a conventional sense. There is, if anything, greater importance in developing the space for all the gifts of the body of Christ in churches for post-Muslims. It speaks of the freeing, renewing work of God, as opposed to the human religious wisdom evident in mosques and in most human institutions.

This affects our worship – developing prayer leadership, giving the chance for all members to pray for others and for specific things. It means that we have to listen carefully to the perspective of all members of the church. It means that we have to support evangelists – going to where they go, listening to how they want to gather their friends, offering support to people quite unlike ordinary church leaders. It means crossing cultural boundaries and thinking through how we run meetings and how we organise the community.

POST-MUSLIMS AND ISLAM

Post-Muslims are, of course, not Muslims. So what's the point of talking to them about Islam? This can be counter-productive. It can be a way of imposing an identity on post-Muslims that they themselves reject.

One reason for doing so is that post-Muslim Christians will rethink their attitude to Islam. Research on post-Muslim Christians shows a pattern: new Christians often reject Islam strongly, both as untrue and immoral.[3] Many later go on to develop a more nuanced view of Islam, retracing their steps and looking at Islam in a different way. A spectacular example of this is Mazhar Mallouhi,[4] a Syrian who rejected Islam as a young man, found Christ, and then moved to a far more sympathetic view of Islam subsequently.

A second reason is that post-Muslims will see strong parallels between Islam and the Old Testament. Many of the key categories are similar: law, circumcision, food taboos, ritual purity, ruling over land, and conquest. If we don't prepare post-Muslims to see where the Old Testament and Islam connect, then they will see those links, possibly in a disordered way. They may assume that the faith of the Bible and of Islam are similar in their endorsement of violence and controlling law.

A third is post-Islam is inherently unstable and it is often a thought-through position. Good disciple-making means equipping Christians with the tools to think about the world, and that world includes Islam. Even if post-Muslims do not hold onto Islamic doctrine or identity, many of the truth questions that Islam asks of Christianity will still echo in their minds. Disciple-makers can model a wise, biblical worldview in the shadow of Islam.

That is related to a fourth reason. Post-Muslims usually have many Muslim friends, family and colleagues. Even if they are no longer asking questions about Islam, their friends will. The questions that Muslims ask are often factual and claim to be logical. If we don't teach about the facts of Christ and also of those who deny

---

[3] See, for example Thomas J. Walsh, "Voices from Christians in Britain with a Muslim Background: Stories for the British Church on Evangelism, Conversion, Integration and Discipleship", MA Thesis for Birmingham Christian College, September 2005 (unpublished).

[4] Paul-Gordon Chandler, *Pilgrims of Christ on the Muslim Road* (Lanham, MD: Rowman & Littlefield, 2008).

him, we may open a door to those who claim to have the intellectual high ground.

Finally, as we've seen above, post-Muslims often hold onto ideas which Islam shares with our most basic religious instincts, such as that people are good, they just need guidance; that life is a test; that God loves good people and rejects bad people. As we teach the gospel, we are teaching that all people are slaves to sin, that no-one is righteous before God, and God saves only by his infinite mercy and grace. We may be unteaching the doctrines of Islam, not in its specifics, but in its basic map of humanity.

So how do we teach about Islam? A lot of this will depend on the individual, including their level of education, and their engagement with Islam in the first place. The main way of teaching about Islam would be through Christian ideas and texts, contrasting them not directly to Islam, but to the underlying map of ideas that post-Muslims hold. We can draw indirect comparisons, for example on the nature of Christian community, or worship. Addressing specifically Muslim issues, such as the origins of the Quran and its relationship to Christian ideas, whether sympathetically or not is another level which may or may not be helpful, depending on the individual. Some post-Muslims are fascinated by this and are only too keen to discuss it, whereas others find it a distraction and would rather relegate any specifically Muslim ideas into the past.

Teaching in the World of Post-Islam

Muslims don't read the Quran in the same way that Christians read the Bible. Christians read the Bible hoping to understand it and gain insight. They are sometimes even open to changing their minds when reading it. Traditionally, Muslims have tended to recite or memorise the Quran, but not interpret it. Interpretation is the work of the educated and the qualified, of imams and scholars. Consequently, Muslims don't offer their opinion on what the Quran might mean. When we teach post-Muslims, it's important to reverse this process. That means offering people the Bible itself, and inviting them to interpret it. Obviously, that doesn't mean that we have to accept any ideas about it. But we should give people the opportunity to read, understand, ask questions and look at the Bible for themselves. That means, on the one hand, avoiding talking over the top of the Bible, threading it through a talk about a topic or a theme of our choosing. On the other hand, even a good, sound, detailed explanation of the Bible may give the impression that reading and understanding the Bible is a job for experts, and that questions aren't welcome.

This may be important too because post-Muslims don't have a lot of the biblical knowledge that we take for granted. Even non-Christians in our society will probably have some grasp of say, the Christmas narrative. This isn't necessarily the case for post-Muslims, who may be genuinely surprised to find out that Mary was engaged to Joseph, for example. Discussion and reacting to questions allow us to slow down and help people work at a pace that suits them. I am constantly struck by how much I have assumed of post-Muslims, and where they have not understood verbal teaching.

One church that I know translates the talks into other languages by simplifying the English into short sentences, machine translating the text, then adding the Bible text from online translations. In the past, this would have been extremely difficult, due to the limitations of machine translation. As long as the English is sufficiently simplified, it is now a useful tool and helps non-English speakers from all backgrounds engage with the text.

CHRIST WITH US: POST-MUSLIM WORSHIP

Post-Muslims are not Muslims – they rarely long for the simple rituals of Islam, and are often quite at home with music in churches, in a way that Muslims are not. Possibly our greatest mistake in worshipping with post-Muslims is low expectations. We can expect the journey to Christ to be slow and cerebral, not revolutionary and powerful. We can be embarrassed about intense worship experiences, or worried that praying with people for any length of time will put them off. Sometimes, our low expectations can be a block to a deeper relationship with Christ in worship. A look at Iranian churches, or Kabyle[5] churches in Algeria often shows a level of fervour that makes the average British church seem rather tame.

---

[5] The Kabyle people are the largest Amazigh or Berber people group in Algeria.

The biggest single lesson then is, quite simply, pray. Pray often and pray with faith, pray out of a relationship with Christ that will be infectious – caught as well as taught. That said, I would suggest encouraging people to pray in their mother tongue, keeping the worship form fairly simple, and using different tools to grow people in worship, including videos, particularly where there is some kind of language barrier.

Muslims usually pray without expectation of a relationship with God, or of really hearing from him. Post-Muslims are not looking, generally, for a repetition of that pattern. The things of the Spirit may be alien to post-Muslims, but that will not make them unattractive.

Conclusion

We started out by looking at what was not. When Islam fades, it leaves a gap, and that gap has a shape. Post-Muslims aren't a cohesive, neatly defined group, and the biggest single lesson from working among them is: don't assume. We cannot assume what people think or what they need. Reaching out to post-Muslims often, is simply a matter of doing the most basic things right: pray, spread the word of God, love deeply. Working with post-Muslims doesn't require a high degree of knowledge about Islam. Often, all it requires is that we raise our expectations of how open to the gospel someone with a Muslim name might be. It might require us to listen, to grasp what people are actually saying, and it might require us to be in the right places, doing the simple work of spreading the gospel.

At a deeper level, we may be aware of the persistence of Islamic thought forms, and the way that they shape reactions to Christian faith. Our challenge then, is not to react to the visible, taught religion of Islam, but often to the persisting assumptions that post-Muslims hold as well as our own assumptions of how they may behave or what they will want. The world is changing quickly. The number of post-Muslims is growing rapidly, and, as it does, so does the challenge and opportunity.

Bibliography

Ali, Ayaan Hirsi. *The Caged Virgin*. London: Simon & Schuster, 2007.

Brown, Daniel W. *Rethinking Tradition in Modern Islamic Thought*. Cambridge: Cambridge University Press, 1999.

Chandler, Paul-Gordon. *Pilgrims of Christ on the Muslim Road*. Lanham, MD: Rowman & Littlefield, 2008.

Conan-Doyle, Arthur. *The Memoirs of Sherlock Holmes*. London: George Newnes, 1894.

Garratón Mateu, Carmen. "Religion et identité amazighe: réflexions sur le rôle de l'islam en Kabylie (Algérie)", In Mohand Tilmatine & Thierry Desrues, Eds. *Les Revendications Amazighes Dans La Tourmente Des «Printemps Arabes»*. Rabat: Centre Jacques-Berque, 2018.

Green, Tim. *Joining the Family*. Birmingham, UK: Kitab / Interserve, 2016.

Holland, Tom. *Dominion: How the Christian Revolution Remade the World*. London: Little Brown, 2019.

Hunter, Shireen T. *Iran, Islam, and the Struggle for Identity and Power in the Islamic Republic of Iran*. ACMCU Occasional Papers Series. Georgetown, Washington DC: Alwaleed Bin Talal Centre for Muslim-Christian Understanding, 2014.

Inglehart, Ronald F. *Religion's Sudden Decline*. Oxford: Oxford University Press, 2021.

Al-Jarhi, Mabid. *The Islamic Political System: A Basic Value Approach*. Kuala Lumpur: INCEIF, 2016.

Kashouh, Hikmat. *Following Jesus in Turbulent Times*. Carlisle: Langham, 2018.

Lewis, Rebecca. "Insider Movements: Honoring God-Given Community and Identity". *International Journal of Frontier Missiology*, 26(1), (Spring 2009): 16–19.

Menk, Mufti. *Motivational Moments*, 1st edition. Singapore: ALQ Creative, 2020.

Muller, Roland. *The Messenger, the Message, the Community: Three Critical Issues for the Cross-Cultural Church-Planter*. Vancouver: CanBooks, 2006.

van Nieuwkerk, Karin. *Understanding Unbelief in Egypt: Report on Preliminary Findings*. Nijmegen, the Netherlands: Radboud University, 2019.

Spellman, Kathryn. *Religion and Nation: Iranian Local And Transnational Networks in Britain*. Oxford: Berghahn, 2005.